FUN & GAMES FOR AGES 1 TO 10

Written by Vicki J. Kuyper
Illustrated by Kristin Kennedy

Edited by Jonna C. Gress
Book Design by Kass Johns

Table of Contents

Everyone loves a party! A successful one, that is. But a child's idea of a successful party may be quite different from your own. The cake may flop, the camera may not flash, and the piñata may burst before anyone has a chance to swing at it, but your child may still say, "Mom, that was the best party ever!"

The key to a "successful" children's party is remembering who the party is for—the kids. Children want fun, giggles, and a few surprises rather than an elaborate celebration. This book contains ideas that will make any party more fun. There are hints for holiday and birthday parties, with a variety of ideas to choose from, depending on the ages of the guests and the time and money you want to spend. Just add your own ideas and enthusiasm, and you're bound to have a party kids will enjoy—and one you'll enjoy, too!

As a parent, it's up to you to oversee the party plans and help get things organized. Start a couple of weeks in advance! First, decide with your child whom to invite and how long the party will be. One rule of thumb is to invite the same number of children as the age in years of your child, plus one or two. Generally, a time limit of ½ to 1 hour for 1- and 2-year-olds, 1½ to 2 hours for 3- to 5-year-olds, 2 to 2½ hours for 6- to 8-year-olds, and 2½ to 3 hours for kids 9 and up is adequate.

Don't forget to plan what siblings will be doing at the time of the party. Unless the age difference is very small, older children usually don't appreciate younger brothers or sisters tagging along during the party activities and don't wish to be included as a "helper" at a younger sibling's party. This is a good time for the sibling who is not part of the party to take a trip to Grandma's or visit a friend.

SETTING THE PARTY MOOD

After figuring out the time, date, and guest list, it's time to come up with invitations. Traditional invitations can be sent through the mail, or hand-delivered by you and your child. Or, your child can be in charge of handing out invitations to his or her friends. Just give a quick phone call to all of the parents of the guests to make sure no invitations were misplaced along the way.

Throughout this book, there are ideas for homemade party invitations your kids may enjoy helping you make. Though it is more expensive, children also enjoy choosing their own party invitations from a store or catalog. If the party is to celebrate a birthday, the choice of invitation can dictate a party theme. Though a theme, such as dinosaurs, animal safari, or a fairy tale is not necessary, it does help give you ideas for decorations and activities, and often gives guests ideas for birthday presents. Even for holiday parties, when the theme is predetermined, there are variations you can do to make a party more unique. (See CHRISTMAS THEME PARTIES, page 20.)

This book also contains ideas for simple decorations that can dress up the party area and add a festive touch to any pictures you will be taking. Use what you have around the house, such as children's toys, instead of spending a lot on a purchased centerpiece and decorations. In general, young children don't really appreciate elaborate party goods. Crepe paper streamers and balloons are sufficient to put them in the party mood. Remember to take a few pictures of the decorations and refreshments *before* the party!

DON'T FORGET THE FOOD!

Along with prizes and favors, refreshments are one of the highlights of a party for children! As with every part of party planning, try to keep it simple. Choose recipes your child likes instead of those you love to prepare.

Stickers that complement the party theme can be stuck on wooden picks and inserted into frosted cupcakes for simple treats. Or, bake **Surprise Cupcakes** by placing gumdrops or other small candies into the batter-filled cupcake paper liners before baking.

Purchased cakes and cookies will be appreciated just as much as an elaborate dessert you've spent hours creating. Once again, your choice ultimately depends on the time and money you want to spend. For new ideas on party refreshments, see the "Munchies" section in each chapter.

Though sweets are traditional party fare, fruits, vegetables, and sandwiches presented in kid-pleasing ways are healthy alternatives. Just keep in mind the purpose of the party—a celebration *kids* will enjoy.

ACTIVITIES

To keep the party moving smoothly, organize it in 15-minute segments. In addition to time for food, favors, and gifts, kids want time to play. Game suggestions are at the end of each chapter and are arranged in order of difficulty. Keep the games easy enough so all the children can have fun playing without getting frustrated.

Children under the age of 4 may have difficulty understanding "winning" and "losing." It may be helpful to end each game by awarding everyone a prize for playing well, letting the "winner" choose first. Or, give small party favors to the other children as the winner opens his or her "special" prize. (See "Prizes and Favors" on the next page.)

If the activities you've planned call for teams, it's important to have a way of selecting teams so no one feels left out. You can have the children **Count Off** ("1-2-1-2-1-2") with the 1s being one team and the 2s the other. Or, you can put an equal number of **Red and Black Checkers** into a hat (totaling the number of children present) and have each child draw a checker assigning them to the red or black team. For more than two teams, you can put **Pieces of Paper in a Hat** in as many colors as you need teams (again including enough to equal the number of children at the party) and have each child choose a paper out of the hat. The old standby of **Drawing Straws** also divides children into two teams, those who choose the short straw and those who choose the long one.

One of the best activities to finish a party is to have a **Clean-Up Race** to music. Put a trash container in the middle of the room and have everyone put in any trash left over from snacks or activities. After the room is clean, give the children their party favors for doing such a good job.

There are several advantages to having parties outside the home, should you decide to do so. Other than inviting the guests, usually your only task is to supervise. You don't need to worry about decorations, activities, or clean-up. Though many kid-oriented places offer parties, check several locations to compare both the services they offer and the price per guest. They can differ considerably.

A few suggested locations for parties outside the home are:

pizza parlor   fast-food restaurant
zoo   ice or roller rink
park   children's museum
miniature golf course   amusement park

PRIZES AND FAVORS

Prizes and favors are an important part of the party for children and they allow everyone to take home a little of the party fun. To avoid problems later, set aside a place where guests can keep their prizes in individual, personalized paper bags. To keep early arrivers occupied, have them decorate their own "booty bag" while waiting for the others to arrive.

With children under the age of 4, it may be easiest to hand out a small favor bag as they are leaving the party. This way, none of the favors are lost and the children do not spend the whole party playing with the goodies in their bags—unless, of course, that's what you want!

Prizes and favors do not need to be expensive to be treasures to a child. Here are a few suggestions:

plastic rings	stickers	plastic animals	small cars
writing pads	paper stars	bean bags	puzzles
balls	crayons	stencils	ribbons
marbles	coloring books	modeling clay	comic books
jacks	change purses	finger puppets	joke books
magnets	water pistols	magic tricks	pencils
bubble pipes	barrettes	fortune cookies	plastic sunglasses

LAST-MINUTE PARTY SAVERS

The children, no matter what the age, will want some unstructured time just to play. But, it's a good idea to have some back-up activities on hand just in case you run out of things to do and the children are becoming bored.

For instance, have on hand easy craft projects, coloring books with a bucket of crayons or a bottle of bubble solution. Don't forget well-known kids' games like **Simon Says, Tic-Tac-Toe,** and **20 Questions. Pin the Tail on the Donkey** is an old favorite that can easily be adapted to many different themes, such as **Pin the Star on the Sheriff** for a Wild West Party or **Pin the Wart on the Witch** for Halloween. Instead of a straight pin, use a rolled piece of masking tape to keep little fingers from getting poked.

Or, create your own version of **Musical Chairs.** For example, place pillows on the floor instead of chairs. When the music stops, encourage the children to squeeze together on the remaining pillows, instead of eliminating children from the game. (See "Musical Presents," page 16, and "Musical Hearts," page 22, for more variations.)

Once again, through all of the planning and the party itself, just remember the party is for the kids . . . then relax and enjoy yourself!

DECORATING IDEAS

Halloween is a favorite time for kids of all ages. It's a time for pretending, goodies, and a shiver or two. A children's Halloween party can be anything from a costumed get-together before trick-or-treating to an elaborately planned time of chills and thrills.

Strobe lights, spooky music, black crepe paper, and a few ghosts made out of sheets are simple ways to set the mood. Jack-o-lanterns are also fun in a darkened room, but for a children's party it's best to put a small flashlight inside a hollowed pumpkin instead of a candle. Very young children can draw faces on an uncut pumpkin with a waterproof felt-tip pen. Remember, children under 5 are easily frightened, so a dangling plastic spider and a few pumpkins in a well-lit room will probably be all the "atmosphere" that is needed.

Invitations can be made from Halloween shapes cut from colored paper, such as a witch's hat, pumpkin, or mask. Party information can also be written on the back of a small trick-or-treat bag which can be brought to the party for treats. Don't forget to write on the invitation whether or not the children are to come in costume!

MUNCHIES

Since Halloween is often centered around candy, providing some fruit punch before or after trick-or-treating may be enough. A refreshing, **Halloween Punch** can be made by combining a large can of pineapple juice, 2 quarts of orange drink, 1 quart of ginger ale, 1 quart of orange sherbet, and 1 small package of orange gelatin. The punch can be served from a bowl placed inside a large, hollowed pumpkin. You can draw a face on the pumpkin with a felt-tip pen, if desired.

Pumpkin cookies or orange cupcakes decorated with faces made from cut black licorice are easy additions if the party will not take place on the same day as the trick-or-treating.

PARTY FUN

Costume Judging

No Halloween party would be complete without costume judging. A costume parade gives everyone a chance to show off their outfits. For children under 4, you can make up enough categories, such as the "prettiest," "spookiest," "most creative," and "funniest," so everyone will win a prize. You can also have a contest for costumes made at the party from paper bags. Let the children cut, paste, and color costumes in teams or individually.

Guess the Ghost

Divide the children into two teams, assigning a spokesperson for each team. The first team leaves the room. Each child on the first team takes a turn putting on a sheet and standing in the doorway making ghost sounds for the second team. The second team discusses who they think the ghost is and their spokesperson announces their final decision. If they are correct, they get one point. After everyone on the first team has had a turn, the second team takes turns playing the ghost. The team with the most points wins.

Bat Race

Before the party, set up two chairs and tie a piece of string to the back of each. (The longer the piece of string, the more difficult the game.) Cut two bat shapes out of black construction paper and make a hole in the top center of each with a hole punch. Thread one bat on each piece of string. At the party, divide the children into two teams. Have the first player of each team stand at the end of the room opposite the chair with the string laying on the floor in front of him or her. At the signal to begin, the player picks up the loose end of the string and tries to get his or her bat to fly to the chair by raising the string in the air. The team who wins the most two-person heats wins the game.

Mummies

Divide the children into pairs and give each pair a roll of toilet paper. Let each pair decide who will be the "mummy" or assign a "mummy" for each team. At the signal to begin, each partner wraps his or her "mummy" in toilet paper from head to toe. The mummy who is most thoroughly covered with toilet paper at the end of three minutes wins.

Touchy-Feely Storytime

Have the children sit in a circle and close their eyes. Repeat the story below while passing the object suggested around the circle.

"Spooky Sam passed away, so we brought his body here today. Here come pieces of his teeth!" (pieces of chalk)

"Now don't be shy, here comes his eye." (grape)

"You don't suppose, this was Sam's nose?" (piece of hot dog)

"Please don't linger, here comes his finger." (large pickle or carrot)

"Better beware, this was Sam's hair!" (cooked spaghetti)

"I know this sounds a little grim, but this was once inside of him!" (pieces of Jello®)

You can finish the game by having the children try to guess what each part of "Spooky Sam" *really* was.

Pumpkin Face Race

Before the party, draw pumpkin shapes on a long sheet of butcher paper or on as many sheets of paper as there will be guests at the party. Tape the paper at the children's eye level along a large wall or hallway. You may want to paper the wall around the drawing area, too, to protect the wall. To begin the race, have the children stand in front of the paper, blindfold each child and give each one a crayon. At the signal to begin, have the children try to draw a face on their pumpkin. After 2 minutes, ask the children to stop and remove their blindfolds. Let the children judge whose pumpkin face is the best.

Make A Monster

Have the children sit in a circle and give each child a magazine to use as a writing surface, a pencil, and a sheet of white paper folded into thirds. Ask everyone to draw a scary monster head on the top third of the paper. Then have the children fold the paper directly beneath the head, hiding the monster head from view. The papers are then passed to the right. Without peeking at the previous artwork, each child now draws a body on the middle third of the page. They then fold this under and pass the paper to the right. Next, each child adds the legs and feet. The papers are then unfolded. Prizes are given to the three co-artists who created the scariest monster.

TRICK-OR-TREATING TIPS

1. Use make-up whenever possible, since a mask hinders a child's vision. Bathtub crayons that wash off with water work well. **Homemade Make-up** can be made by mixing together 1 tablespoon of soft shortening, 2 tablespoons cornstarch, and food color.

2. Use light-colored costumes; fluorescent tape can be placed on costumes to make them more visible in the dark.

3. Check costumes to make sure they're not too long or bulky so children can walk without tripping.

4. Make a quick and easy dinner of favorite finger-foods to serve to kids before they go trick-or-treating. They'll be less tempted to eat all of the goodies they receive if they've had a nourishing dinner first.

5. Always chaperone the trick-or-treating of children under the age of 8. Encourage older children to go with a buddy or two.

6. Provide a flashlight for each child.

7. Stay in a familiar neighborhood and only visit houses where the porch light is on.

8. Inspect all treats before letting children eat them.

9. Instruct children to always walk on the sidewalks and to cross streets at appropriate intersections or crosswalks.

DECORATING IDEAS

Whether you're having a children's party, or just want to help the kids enjoy themselves at your family get-together, here are a few ways to liven up the festivities!

Fun-to-make Thanksgiving decorations are a great party activity that children can take home for their own family celebration. The activity will also keep your children busy while you are trying to prepare the holiday meal!

Turkey Pictures can be made by tracing around a child's hand, adding feet, and then coloring the picture. (See Diagram 1.)

Diagram 1

Make a **Paper Plate Turkey** by making two small cuts at the bottom of a paper plate along the solid lines, as shown in Diagram 2. Fold the cut flap along the dotted lines to make the turkey's head. (See Diagram 3.) Either color in eyes, or glue on jiggly eyes bought at a craft store. Glue or staple real feathers, or ones cut from colored paper, around the top edges of the plate for a colorful wall decoration.

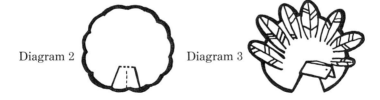

Diagram 2   Diagram 3

You can also make **Thumbprint Place Cards** for the Thanksgiving table by gently pressing a child's thumb against an ink pad and then pressing it onto a folded index card. With crayons or markers, children can draw on the turkey's head, legs, and tail feathers and print a guest's name, or their own, on the place card. (See Diagram 4.) These can also be used as invitations for a Thanksgiving party.

Diagram 4

Children can make a **Thanksgiving Tablecloth** by coloring their own version of the first Thanksgiving on a piece of butcher paper large enough to cover the table or on shelf paper to use as a table runner. Add a little color to the holiday table by having children draw funny faces with felt-tip pens on small gourds, or cutting "autumn leaves" out of colored paper. Then let the children arrange them into a centerpiece or scatter them around the table.

MUNCHIES

If your party does not include the full traditional meal, simple party fare can be pumpkin-flavored cookies or muffins decorated with candy corn. Or, make some homemade "Pilgrim Candy." (See recipe below.) Warm apple cider or hot cocoa makes a tummy-warming complement.

PARTY FUN

Stuff That Turkey!

Give each child a clean men's athletic sock, a spoon, and a bowl of popped popcorn. At the signal to begin, each child must stuff his or her "turkey" (the sock) with spoonfuls of popcorn. After 2 minutes the most well-stuffed turkey wins.

Pilgrim Candy Pull

Make candy just like the pilgrims did by combining 2 cups of honey, 1 cup of sugar, and 1 cup of heavy cream. Cook slowly until a small piece of the mixture turns into a hard ball when dropped into cold water. (This is best done before the party.) At the party, when the candy is cool enough to handle, spread butter on everyone's hands and have them pull the candy mixture until it's a golden color. Cut it in pieces and let the children wrap them in squares of waxed paper to take home. The fun is well worth the mess!

Butterball Boogie

Divide the children into pairs; give each pair a cup of whipping cream in a jar, making sure the lids are screwed on tightly. Have the children in each pair take turns shaking the jar until the whipping cream forms a ball of butter. The first pair to finish wins. To finish the butter so the children can take it home for their holiday celebrations, pour off the liquid and add a dash of salt to each jar. Yellow food color may be added, if desired. Use a spoon to mix and press excess liquid out of the butter.

FAMILY CELEBRATION TIPS

1. Have a special Thanksgiving table just for children. It needn't be fancy; a card table set up in a corner of the dining room or a vinyl tablecloth set out on the kitchen floor will do fine. Use paper plates for easy clean-up. The children can decorate the rims with Thanksgiving stickers while they are waiting, if you wish.

2. Plan activities such as making decorations (see "Decorating Ideas," page 12) or playing a special video to keep the children entertained while you are preparing the meal.

3. Help children understand the meaning of the holiday by having them state one thing they're thankful for before they begin their meal. Help them develop a "Thanksgiving attitude" before Thanksgiving by making a paper chain with fourteen links. Two weeks prior to Thanksgiving, have the children remove one link every evening and say something they were thankful for that day.

4. Children don't enjoy sitting at the table for long periods of time, so while the adults are finishing their dinner, ask the children to work on their own play about Thanksgiving. Provide a variety of old clothes for costumes. After the adults are finished with dinner, they can be the audience for the children's show.

DECORATING IDEAS

One of the advantages of having a party at this time of year is that your house is already decorated and ready for holiday fun. A Christmas tree and cookies make any home ready for a party.

Party invitations can be just a note inserted in a Christmas card. Or, children may enjoy making invitations by cutting out one of the many Christmas symbols from colored paper. A round piece of paper decorated with crayons, sequins, stickers, or old cut-up Christmas cards makes an easy Christmas ornament invitation. The party information can be written on the back. Or, have the children cut white paper into wide candy-cane shapes, color in the red stripes, and write party information on the alternating white stripes. Christmas trees, stockings, or gingerbread people can also be cut out of colored paper and decorated by you or your child.

MUNCHIES

Christmas cookies are an all-time favorite, and children can decorate their own cookies as part of the party fun. Children 2 and up will enjoy decorating sugar or gingerbread cookie shapes that you've cut out before the party. Cover a large table with a washable tablecloth and set out bowls of raisins, coconut, small candies, and sprinkles. If you're not too concerned about the aesthetics of the cookie, or the mess in the kitchen, this can be a lot of fun.

Having a **Cookie Exchange** cuts down on the time you need to prepare snacks for the party. On the invitation, request that each child bring a dozen of his or her family's favorite Christmas cookies. This is not only easy on the hostess, but a great way to find new holiday recipes.

A **Snowman Cake** is an easy and festive treat. Just place two round cakes next to each other on a large piece of cardboard covered with foil wrapping paper. Frost the cakes with white icing and sprinkle them with coconut. Create a snowman face with candy or colored frosting.

Make **Snowman Cupcakes** by topping white frosted cupcakes with "snowmen" made of two large marshmallows stacked on a wooden pick. (Use the wooden picks only with children over 4.) Cupcakes can also be decorated with green-tinted icing and sprinkled with small red candies.

A few cinnamon candies in the bottom of a cup of hot cider or cocoa make a delicious and quick holiday beverage.

PARTY FUN

Musical Presents

Before the party, wrap a small present in ten or more layers of paper, fastening each layer with masking tape. To begin the game, have the children sit in a circle. Turn on some music and have the children quickly pass the present around the circle. Stop the music at frequent intervals. Each time the music stops, the child holding the package unwraps one layer of paper. The child who unwraps the final layer of paper wins the present.

Ornament Odyssey

Hide Christmas ornaments around the party area. Give each child a box and set a timer for 5 minutes. Have the children search for hidden ornaments, placing the ones they find in their box. At the end of the game, the children can decorate a tree at the party or take their ornaments home to decorate their own tree. A prize can be given for the most ornaments found.

All I Want For Christmas

Give everyone a piece of colored paper cut in the shape of a Christmas stocking. Place old Christmas catalogs and children's blunt-tipped safety scissors in the middle of the room. (For small children, place pre-cut pictures of toys in the middle of the floor or table.) Ask the children to find pictures of things they'd like for Christmas and then glue the items onto their stockings. This makes a "Christmas wish list" small children can take home to their parents.

Stuff the Stocking

Divide the children into teams and seat them on the floor. Give the first member of each team a Christmas stocking and an identical number of small gifts. At the signal to begin, have the players stuff the stocking with all of the gifts and then hand the filled stocking to the next player on their team. That player empties the stocking and fills it again with the gifts, passing it on to the next player, and so on down the line. The team that finishes first wins.

Christmas Greetings

Seat the children in a circle and designate one child to be Santa. Santa goes to the center of the circle, then chooses a child in the circle and says, "Merry Christmas and a Happy New Year!" Before Santa finishes speaking, the child he is speaking to must reply, "The same to you!" or the two change places. If, however, the child addressed by Santa answers within the time given, Santa must move on to someone else in the circle.

Human Christmas Trees

Divide the children into teams. Have two children from each team stand back-to-back with their arms out and one leg extended to simulate branches of a Christmas tree. Give the rest of the children decorations, such as tinsel, garlands, strings of popcorn, and a few ornaments with a loop of string tied to the top instead of a metal hanger. Set a timer for 3 minutes. The team with the most unique "tree" wins. You may want to play this game several times so each child has a chance to be the tree.

The Toy Shop

Place a dozen or more toys on a table. Ask one player to go out of the room. While the player is gone, ask someone to remove a toy and hide it. Then have the child that has left the room return and try to guess which toy is missing. That child then designates someone to leave the room and, if he or she has guessed correctly, has the fun of hiding the next toy. Make sure every child has a turn to guess the missing toy.

Clothesline Greetings

Before the party, cut out two sets of large letters to spell out "Merry Christmas." To begin the game, divide the children into two teams and give each team a clothesline, clothespins, and one set of letters. Let each team choose two children to hold up the clothesline. At the signal to begin, have the designated children hold the clothesline taut while the others pin up the letters to spell "Merry Christmas." A prize can be given for the fastest, or neatest job. "Clothesline Greetings" can be great fun for other occasions: "Happy Valentine's Day," "Happy Thanksgiving," and "Happy Birthday."

Gift Exchanges

There are many different ways to have a child's gift exchange at a party. With a **Traditional Gift Exchange** each child brings a small gift worth a certain value ($1 or $2 is usually adequate to buy a small gift, yet still will not hinder anyone from attending the party). As the children enter, have each one put his or her gift under the tree. After munchies and party games, assign a number to each child. Then, beginning with Number 1, and going in order, have each child pick a gift from under the tree.

With a **Merry-Go-Round Gift Exchange**, the children sit in a circle, holding the gifts they brought. While a Christmas carol plays, have the children pass the gifts to the right. Stop the music and then begin it again, but this time have the children pass the gifts to the left. Stop the music again and then pass the gifts once more to the right. When the music stops, have the children shout "Merry Christmas!" and open the package they're holding.

For a **Hidden Gift Exchange**, wrap a gift for each child coming to the party, or designate on each child's invitation the person for whom he or she is responsible for buying a gift. Make sure all gifts are labeled and no one is left out. Hide the gifts throughout the party area. To begin the search, explain that each child may only take the gift that has his or her name on it and may not reveal the location of anyone else's gift.

A **White Elephant Gift Exchange** is similar to the Traditional Gift Exchange, except that everyone is encouraged to bring a gag gift or a "white elephant" from their home. Each child is assigned a number. Number 1 chooses a gift and opens it. Number 2 may either choose an unopened gift from under the tree or take the gift from Number 1. If he or she takes the gift already opened, Number 1 gets to choose another gift from under the tree. Number 3 can then choose between the two gifts already opened or choose an unopened gift from under the tree, and so on. Older children really enjoy the fun of this gift exchange. It's a nice surprise at the end to give a special prize for the person stuck with the worst gag gift.

Christmas Theme Parties

Besides having a gift exchange, there are also a variety of themes you can use to make your party a little bit different. A **Red and Green Party** theme can be carried out in everything from invitations to munchies. In your invitations (out of red and green colored paper, of course), ask all the children to wear either red or green. They can also bring a small present for a gift exchange wrapped in red or green paper. The gift could also be either red or green. Decorate the party area with red and green streamers and follow the theme with frozen strawberries floating in a bowl of limeade punch. Frost cupcakes with white icing tinted with a few drops of red or green food color. For the very adventurous, tint the cupcakes with green food color before baking; top with cherry frosting when cooled. Kids will love it!

Older children who understand the importance of "giving" at Christmastime will enjoy a **Giving Party**. The party can be a special time of getting together and making homemade gifts, cards, ornaments, or cookies, and then visiting a hospital or convalescent home to hand out the homemade goodies and sing carols. This can even be done in your own neighborhood, where the children sing carols for the neighbors and deliver homemade treats. With all of the "receiving" at Christmastime, this is a nice party alternative.

To help young children understand the religious significance of Christmas, you can have a **Birthday Party for Jesus.** If the number of children at the party is small, everyone can help bake and frost a cake. Microwave cake mixes only take about 10 minutes to mix and bake and will keep the party activities moving. Let the kids decorate the cake and sing "Happy Birthday" to Jesus. You can also incorporate a special kind of gift exchange. Ask each child to think of something he or she would like to do for Jesus by helping another person. Examples could be helping Mom dry the dishes or lending a favorite toy to a brother or sister. Help the children write the idea on a slip of paper and wrap it in a small box. These can either be placed in front of a crèche at home or given to the person for whom the special deed will be done.

DECORATING IDEAS

Purchased or handmade valentines can play a big part at a Valentine's Day party, not only as favors or gifts to make, but as invitations and decorations. Children can invite their friends to the party by putting the party information on the back of a valentine. Valentines can also be used as place cards at the table and hung from streamers to decorate the party area.

Unique valentines can also be woven from colored paper. Cut one piece of red paper and one piece of white paper into the shape shown in Diagram 1. Cut ten even-sized strips into the bottom of both pieces of paper. (See Diagram 1.) Weave the paper at right angles to one another, making a heart. (See Diagram 2.) Paste or tape each end securely and trim any uneven sections. Make these any size, from tiny, carefully woven name tags to large place mats or wall decorations.

Diagram 1    Diagram 2

MUNCHIES

Heart-shaped cinnamon candies or conversation candy hearts can be used to decorate any type of cake or cookie. **Heart-shaped Cupcakes** can be made by dropping a small marble between each batter-filled cupcake paper liner and the muffin-tin cups before baking.

Or bake some **Heart Tarts** by rolling pre-made pie dough ⅛" thick and cutting it into heart shapes with a cookie cutter. Place half of the hearts on a cookie sheet and top each with a teaspoon of raspberry jam. Cover with a matching pre-cut dough heart, seal the edges, and prick with a fork. Bake at 450° for 10 to 12 minutes. Remove from the oven, set on a wire rack to cool, and sprinkle with red candied sugar.

Turn any cold drink into **Sweetheart Punch** by putting red sour balls or heart-shaped gel candy into the compartments of an ice cube tray. Fill with water and freeze. Put the special ice cubes into your favorite red punch.

PARTY FUN

Who's My Valentine?

Before the party, cut purchased valentines in half at odd angles. To play the game, give each child half a valentine, making sure that another child has the matching half. At the signal to begin, the children try to find the matching half of the valentine they have and then sit down. The first pair to sit down wins.

Musical Hearts

Before the party, cut out heart-shaped pieces of cardboard of various sizes. Place the hearts on the floor around the party area. The game is played like musical chairs, only when the music stops everyone must stand on a heart. It's okay to share a heart. Before each round, take away one heart, so it becomes more difficult for everyone to share the available hearts. Anyone who is not on a heart when the music stops is out. Leave out the smallest heart shape for the last round. This game can also be used for Halloween with pumpkin shapes, birthday parties with balloon shapes, and so on.

Broken Hearts

Before the party, cut a paper heart into pieces like a jigsaw puzzle. (You'll need one heart for each guest.) Put each heart puzzle into an envelope. At the signal to begin, have each child put together his or her heart. The first one to finish wins a prize. The difficulty of the game can be determined by the number of pieces and complexity of their shapes, depending on the age of the partygoers.

Hang Onto Your Heart!

Give each child two saucers and two straws. Put five conversation candy hearts (or cinnamon heart candies, if you want the game to be more difficult) into one of the saucers. At the signal to begin, each child has to use his or her straws as chopsticks, picking up one piece of candy at a time and transporting it to the other saucer, about 5 inches away. If it's dropped between the two saucers, the candy must be picked up by hand, put back into the first saucer, and the player must start over. The first player to get all of his or her hearts in the second saucer wins. As a variation, divide the children into relay teams.

Love Messages

Before the party, make or purchase two sets of three identical valentines and put each set into an envelope. To begin the game, divide the children into teams and have each team stand on one side of the room facing each other. At the signal to begin, have the first member of each team take the valentines out of the envelope and read them as loudly, quickly, and accurately as possible. After the first member finishes, he or she puts the valentines back into the envelope and passes them on to the next member, and so on down the line. The first team that finishes wins. The difficulty of this game depends on the complexity of the verse on the valentines. The older the children, the longer and more complex the verse can be.

Candy Charades

Fill a bowl with conversation candy hearts which have short sayings such as "I Love You," "Be Mine," and "Sealed With A Kiss." Each child takes a turn to select one of the candies and tries to pantomime its message. If someone correctly guesses the message within the chosen time frame, the "mime" gets to eat the candy. You can play this game with teams, giving a prize to the team who guesses the most answers in the least amount of time; or you can let each child take a turn in front of the group.

DECORATING IDEAS

At Eastertime, decorating can be as simple as placing stuffed bunnies and Easter eggs around the party area. An Easter basket filled with flowers and dyed eggs makes a nice centerpiece for the table. Dyed eggs can also be used as "place cards." If you write the child's name in white crayon on the hard-boiled egg before dyeing it, the name will remain white when the egg is dyed.

A personalized **Bunny Bag** to hold party goodies or collect Easter eggs can be made from a small paper sack. Cut bunny ears from the open end of a small white, flattened bakery sack (or colorful lunch bag) as shown in Diagram 1. Staple the top of each ear together. Draw a simple bunny face on the bag and then unfold. (See Diagram 2.) Glue a cotton ball bunny tail on the back of each bag and fill with treats or small gifts. The bunny bag can also be used to collect goodies found during an Easter egg hunt.

Diagram 1 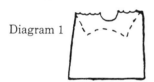   Diagram 2

For fun and easy invitations, give plastic eggs to each potential party guest with the party information written on a slip of paper tucked inside.

MUNCHIES

Since there are usually plenty of sweets involved in Easter activities, it is a good idea to offer a nutritious snack during the party such as "bunny food"—carrot sticks and dip or celery filled with cream cheese or peanut butter.

Egg-shaped Cookies can also be made by removing both ends from an empty frozen juice can and gently squeezing it into an oval shape. Use your home-made cookie cutter to cut "eggs" from your favorite rolled cookie dough recipe. Decorate with pastel icing, if desired.

Pink lemonade or milk tinted with pink food color are good party beverages. If the weather is still more like winter than spring, float a chocolate-covered egg in a cup of hot cocoa.

PARTY FUN

Captain Bunny

For a change in the traditional Easter Egg Hunt, try Captain Bunny. Divide the children into two teams and draw straws to choose a captain for each team. With younger children, have an adult act as captain. The children must find one egg at a time and bring it to their captain before they continue their search for more eggs. After all the eggs are found, the team whose captain has the most eggs wins.

Jelly Bean Exchange

Give each child at the party a small basket, or use a "bunny bag" (see page 24) containing a dozen different colored jelly beans. The goal is to get as many of the same color of jelly beans as possible. Set a timer for 3 minutes and let the children exchange jelly beans. The player who ends up with the most jelly beans of one color wins. For younger children, you may want to pick a specific color for each child, but older children will have fun choosing their own colors.

Bunny Tail Boogie

Give each child a straw, a small bowl and an equal number of cotton balls. At the signal to start, each child puts the straw in his or her mouth and tries to pick up a cotton ball by sucking into the opposite end of the straw. The child then drops the cotton ball into the bowl, continuing until all of his or her "bunny tails" are in the bowl. The first player to finish wins. This game can also be played as a timed relay with teams. This is best for children ages 5 and up.

Jelly Bean Drop

Give each child an equal number of jelly beans. Have each child take a turn kneeling on a chair and dropping jelly beans into a partially opened milk carton. The player who drops the most jelly beans into the milk carton wins. This game is easy to adapt to different age groups by adjusting the size of the target or the distance it is placed from the player's chair. Have older children drop their jelly beans into muffin-tin cups for added difficulty, counting only the ones that don't bounce out. Award a prize to the winner or let the jelly beans be the prize!

Easter Bonnet Parade

For this Easter Bonnet Parade, you'll need ten old hats and two chairs. Divide the children into two teams. Place five hats next to each chair. Start the children on the opposite side of the room. Each child must hurry to the other end of the room, put on a hat, go around the chair and then remove the hat. The children must do this with each of the five hats, then quickly return to their team where the next in line takes his or her turn. The first team to complete their parade wins.

Feather Up!

This is a simple game for all ages. You will need a stopwatch with a second hand and several feathers. The object is to keep the feathers in the air by blowing on them. This game can be played with the children divided into pairs or in small groups with a leader. (Use an adult as the leader for very young children.) In the group game, everyone holds hands while the leaders each throw a feather into the air above their groups. The group, or pair, that keeps its feather in the air the longest wins.

Easter Egg Roll

You will need a hard-boiled, dyed Easter egg for each child. Divide the children into small teams. The object is for each team member to roll an Easter egg across the room to the finish line with his or her nose. The team that finishes first wins.

A Tisket A Tasket,
Jelly Beans In A Basket

Have the children sit in a circle and give each child a bag containing a dozen jelly beans. Pick one person to start. The child puts his or her hand in the bag and takes out some jelly beans. The person to the left guesses how many jelly beans that player has. If the answer is correct, the player keeps the jelly beans, if the answer is incorrect, that player gives the person on the left the difference in jelly beans from his or her bag. Go around the circle completely three times. The player with the least jelly beans at the end of the game wins.

"Eggs"tra Surprises

This is an excellent game for small children, and works well to close the party. You will need as many plastic eggs as there are guests. (Note: The plastic eggs used to hold pantyhose are larger than most other plastic Easter eggs and work especially well to hold "eggs"tra goodies.) Let each child choose an egg from a large bag. Inside the egg is a number which corresponds to a small, wrapped and numbered gift in an Easter basket. For very small children, place a piece of pink or green paper inside the egg, and the child can choose a small gift from a corresponding pink or green basket.

Party Tips for One-to Three-Year-Olds

Though the first few birthdays of a little one's life are special landmarks for the parents, very young children have no concept of what a party is, let alone a birthday. With a little bit of planning, a simple celebration can still be a special day for you and your child.

THE FIRST BIRTHDAY

The first birthday is really a celebration *of* the child *for* the parents and relatives. Other children may be invited, but at this age they really won't interact much except to try and take away toys from one another.

Your 1-year-old will enjoy colorful streamers and balloons and gaily wrapped packages. As a matter of fact, the wrapping paper may provide more fun than the gifts themselves! Remember, balloons are dangerous toys for children of this age. Bring out a brightly colored beach ball to offer as a playtime alternative. Playing with wrapping paper and ribbons may be all the party "activities" your child will want. Just make sure to keep a close watch so the paper and cards don't become part of the party munchies!

Your child will enjoy almost any type of munchie at this age, as much to play with as to eat. Though a beautifully frosted birthday cake can become quite a mess once attacked by a 1-year-old, it does make memorable photos.

THE SECOND BIRTHDAY

Two-year-olds are an interesting combination of baby and toddler, acting grown-up one minute and the next dissolving into tears. For the second birthday, your child might enjoy having two or three friends over, but the children will probably enjoy playing *next* to each other more than *with* each other. Invite parents to stay with their children at the party to help keep the little ones happy. You can plan simple activities, such as coloring or playing with stickers, or just set out a variety of toys for the children to play with in the party area.

Present-opening time can be traumatic for 2-year-old guests who don't understand why they have to give up the presents they brought. It helps to give each guest a small, wrapped favor to open while the birthday child is opening his or her presents.

Children are very messy at this age, so try and keep refreshments easy to eat. A great way to serve cake to young children is to make **Cake Cones**. Place flat-bottomed ice cream cones on a baking sheet or in muffin-tin cups; fill cones halfway with cake batter. (For a special surprise, put a maraschino cherry in the cone before adding the batter.) Bake according to the cupcake directions on the cake mix box. The cones can be frosted or decorated as desired.

THE THIRD BIRTHDAY

Most children this age will be ready for a more "traditional" party, if it is kept simple and fairly unstructured. Three-year-olds have a short attention span and lack the social skills to play most organized group games. However, you can set up the party area with a variety of simple "country fair"-type activities. Be sure to invite a few of the parents to stay and help out.

A good game for this age group is the old favorite, **Clothespin Drop.** Cover a clean milk carton with construction paper and decorate it with stickers. Most 3-year-olds can have some success with this game. Toss **Bean Bags** into a basket or trash can. Make bean bags by partially filling socks with dried beans and tying off the open end. Very young children don't really understand "winning" and "losing," so award prizes to everyone for trying.

Since present-opening time often holds the same problems as with 2-year-olds, make sure everyone has something to open. Your 3-year-old may have a hard time sharing the new birthday toys with other children. To take everyone's mind off of the new gifts, serve the refreshments as soon as the gifts have been opened!

At the age of 3, a cake with candles to blow out is a real treat. Have some matches handy in case the party guests blow out the candles for the birthday child. Use a paper tablecloth and partyware for easy clean-up.

When it comes to wrapping children's packages, a little imagination goes a long way. Instead of using a box and wrapping paper, try placing the gift in a decorative cookie tin that can be used later to hold crayons, blocks, or small toys long after the gift has been opened. If the gift is small, place it inside a sand pail and tie the shovel to the handle of the pail with some colorful ribbon. If your child is bringing a gift to a friend's party, he or she can decorate plain paper or bags with stickers, crayons, or fingerpaints!

Here are a few more ideas to wrap up special party gifts:

FUN WRAPPING PAPER

newspaper	newspaper comic pages
fabric remnants	foil
plastic bags tied with ribbons	lunch bags
grocery bags	butcher paper

PACKAGE TOPPERS

Decorate a package with extra surprises by tying a package topper onto the gift. Here are a few suggestions:

balloons   colorful shoelaces
hair ribbons   crayons
barrettes   costume jewelry
lollipops   whistles
jump ropes   kazoos
bubble pipes   kid's sunglasses
party noisemakers   cute pencils

You don't have to have a birthday cake to sing "Happy Birthday," make a wish and blow out birthday candles! There are many other imaginative alternatives that can add a little fun to your child's birthday.

Try putting candles in donuts, hot dogs, watermelon or pizza slices. Make homemade ice cream and serve it with lit sparklers instead of traditional birthday candles.*

Some party treats, like popcorn or cookies, aren't well-suited to holding candles. But if that's what your child would like to have, don't let that stop you from serving them at the party! Your child can still have the fun of blowing out birthday candles if you make a **Special Birthday Centerpiece**. Simply fill a shallow bowl with sand, add some small rocks to create a miniature landscape, and decorate it with small toy figures to create a scene: plastic cowboys and Indians for a Wild West Party or tiny toy dinosaurs for a Prehistoric Party. Place the figures to the front of the bowl and the candles to the back to keep the flames away from the toy figures. Or, make a **Candle Bouquet** by putting candles in plastic candle holders and placing them into a flower pot filled with sand or dirt. Your child will enjoy helping create his or her own special centerpiece, as well as blowing out the candles on the "cake" before the other refreshments are served.

*Use extreme caution when using candles or sparklers around little ones. Make sure an adult is always in the room until the candles or sparklers are safely extinguished and removed.

Party Planning Checklist ✔

Party date: _____ Time: _____

Place: _____ Theme: _____

BEFORE THE PARTY

Guest List:

Name	Address	Phone	RSVP

Adults who can help:

Name	Address	Phone

PARTY NEEDS

Supplies/Food	Have	Make	Purchase
invitations			
balloons			
streamers			
other decorations:			
tablecloth			
plates			
cups			
napkins			
forks and spoons			
place mats			
cake			
beverage			
other munchies:			
candles			
matches			
favors and prizes:			
camera			
film			
wrapping paper			
craft and game supplies:			

DECORATING IDEAS

Everyone loves a trip to the circus and kids will have a lot of fun with a circus party theme. You can make your own "Big Top" by decorating the party area with a canopy of crepe paper streamers and placing stuffed animals around the room. With a felt-tip pen, write the guests' names on helium-filled balloons; tie the balloons to the backs of the chairs at the party table, making them "place cards."

Make circus invitations by cutting 2″ balloon shapes from different colors of construction paper. Glue a piece of yarn to the back of each balloon. Arrange and glue the balloons, overlapping slightly, onto a 3 x 5 card. Cover card completely with the balloons. Gather the yarn together and tie into a loose knot. Write the party information on the balloons, using separate balloons for time, date, place, and RSVP. Or, you can insert a small, tightly rolled piece of paper with the party information written on it into a real balloon before inflating. After the balloons are inflated and tied, your child can have the fun of delivering the blown-up balloon invitations, and the recipients will have the fun of popping the balloons to discover the party information. Boxes of animal crackers with the party information tucked inside make unique and yummy invitations as well!

MUNCHIES

Simple refreshments can be bags of peanuts and popcorn, or boxes of animal crackers, and a cup of soda. Use animal-shaped cookie cutters to make **Circus Sandwiches.** An ordinary bologna and cheese sandwich takes on new appeal in an elephant shape.

A **Circus Train Cake** adds a fun touch and it's so easy, too! Bake at least three mini-loaf cakes, frost them, add round candy for wheels, and put animal crackers along the sides of each car to look like a circus train. Cover the refreshment table with circus theme gift wrap, lay a licorice railroad track around the table, and carefully place the "cars" on the track. You can be as elaborate as you want: add a marshmallow smokestack on the engine, pipe "cage bars" in frosting over the animal crackers—use your imagination!

Clown Cupcakes are less work, but still lots of fun. Put scoops of ice cream on baked and cooled cupcakes. Using whatever candy you wish, create faces on the ice cream clown "heads." Top off the cupcakes with sugar-cone hats, and the clowns are ready to entertain your hungry guests!

PARTY FUN

Just Clowning Around

Set aside some time for face painting at your party. (See "Trick-or-Treating Tips" on page 11 for some easy make-up ideas.) Younger children can have their faces painted by the adults present (dressed up in clown outfits if possible). Older children might like to paint their own faces, and you can give a prize for the funniest, happiest, and saddest clown. For take-home souvenirs, take individual pictures of each guest with an instantly developing camera. If you don't want to bother with the mess of make-up, children can color clown faces on white paper plates decorated with orange yarn "hair." Either way, "Just Clowning Around" will be fun for kids of all ages.

Capture the Animals!

Before the party, hide small stuffed animals or miniature plastic circus animals around the party area. Give each child at the party a shoebox with instructions to color the sides of the box to look like a cage. At the signal to begin, ask the children to see how many animals they can capture that have escaped from the circus train! The child who captures the most animals wins.

Balloon Hockey Relay

Divide the children into two teams. Place two chairs at the opposite end of the room. Give the first child in each team a broom and a balloon. The object is to sweep the balloon across the room, around the chair, then back to the next player on the team, who repeats the action. The first team to successfully complete the relay wins.

Balloon Stomp

Divide the children into teams and assign each team a color. The number of teams can be determined by the number and age of children at the party—the more teams, the more complex the game. Give each team an equal number of inflated balloons in their assigned color. At the signal to begin, the team releases the balloons onto the floor and then tries to pop the balloons of opposing colors while defending their own. After the designated time, the team with the most balloons of their color remaining wins.

Monkey Munching

Give each child a banana. At the signal to begin, the children must peel their bananas and eat them while keeping one of their hands behind their backs. The best "monkey" who finishes his or her banana in the least amount of time wins a whole bunch of bananas.

Let It Blow!

Divide the children into teams and give each team member a deflated balloon. With masking tape, mark a goal line at the opposite end of the room. The object is to get the balloon across the goal line by blowing it up, then releasing it, and letting it fly—hopefully—toward the goal. At the signal to begin, the first member of each team blows up his or her balloon, releases it, then hurries to wherever it lands, blows it up again and releases it. This sequence is repeated until the balloon lands across the finish line. The player then runs back and tags the next team member who continues the relay with his or her balloon. The team that gets all of its deflated balloons across the finish line first wins. This is a good game for children over the age of 6. To make the balloons easier to inflate, have the children blow up and deflate their balloons several times before giving the signal to begin.

DECORATING IDEAS

A Dress-up Tea Party is a special time for children to play "grown-up." Though most of the party ideas in this chapter are designed for all-girl parties, they can be adapted for boy/girl parties as well. Most boys 6 years and under enjoy dressing up in their father's ties and sport coats for a "formal" play occasion as much as little girls like donning their mother's dresses and heels.

Write invitations on a tea-cup shape cut from construction paper and pasted onto a paper doily. Invite the children to come in costume or provide a large bag of old clothes and let the children choose a party outfit. Girls can be invited to bring their dolls, dressed for the occasion of course! Children will also enjoy making their own special movie in costume, with you as the video cameraman. Watching a video tape of the tea party is a fun party activity for the children. The video tape makes a wonderful keepsake for your entire family.

Half of the fun of the party is the pretending. Call each guest by their "proper" title of "Mr." or "Miss" when they arrive, as well as throughout the party. You can also add to the fun by acting out the part of the "maid" during the tea party itself.

The refreshment area is the main focus of any tea party. Fix a child-size table for the guests with a disposable or washable tablecloth and children's play dishes. A small arrangement such as a flower centerpiece adds a grown-up touch.

Costume Creations

Children will enjoy adding special touches to their fancy outfits by making their own accessories. Here are a few ideas:

Have the children make their own **Newspaper Hats.** Fold a double sheet of newspaper or computer paper in half, with the open end toward the bottom. (See Diagram 1.) Fold the top two corners toward the center as shown in Diagram 2. Fold the bottom edges up to form a brim and staple the corners together. (See Diagram 3.) Let the guests decorate their hats with feathers, sequins, stickers, or their own crayon or felt-tip pen artwork.

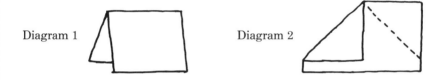

Diagram 1 Diagram 2

Children can also cut **Crowns** out of construction paper or metallic-colored cardboard. (See Diagram 4.) From a 5-inch strip of paper or cardboard, cut one edge in zigzag fashion, fit the crown around the child's head to size, remove and staple or tape the ends together. These crowns can be decorated like the Newspaper Hats, or the children can make "jewels" out of aluminum foil and glue them onto their crowns.

Diagram 3 Diagram 4

To make **Shoelace Necklaces**, string macaroni on extra-long shoelaces. Or, using a large, blunt needle threaded with dental floss, string cut-up licorice pieces and "O"-shaped breakfast cereal to make **Edible Necklaces.**

To make **Shrinking Jewelry**, have the children draw a design with felt-tip pens on a Styrofoam® lid, egg carton, or meat tray. Cut out the design in the desired shape and make a hole at the top of the design with a hole punch. Then crumple and open a piece of aluminum foil and place the plastic design on it. Place both in a preheated 350° to 400° oven and bake for 1 to 2 minutes and watch the design shrink! Carefully remove from the oven, discard the foil, and flatten the design with a book. Let it cool. Thread a piece of yarn through the hole to make a necklace or bracelet. This activity requires adult supervision.

MUNCHIES

For refreshments, you can either serve the children goodies you've prepared ahead of time, or have them help you make the treats as part of the party fun.

Peanut butter and jelly sandwiches cut with cookie cutters and celery sticks filled with cream cheese and raisins make dainty finger food. To make fancy **Egg Boats**, stick a wooden pick through a small "sail" of triangular paper and insert it into the top of a deviled egg "boat." Use apple juice for "tea" and serve it to the children from a pretty teapot.

PARTY FUN

Grown-Up Costume Contest

Have a parade to show off the guests' formal attire. Give a prize to the "Fanciest," "Most Grown-Up," and "Best-Dressed Mother and Baby Doll." Children will also enjoy having a picture of themselves to take home after the party.

"Take It Away!" Memory Game

Place eight to fifteen small objects on a fancy serving tray. (The number of objects will determine the difficulty of the game.) Place a large cloth napkin over the tray to cover the objects. Give each child a pencil and paper. Bring the covered tray into the room and remove the napkin. Give the children a minute to look at the objects before you recover the tray. After the tray is recovered, the children write down the names of the objects they remember seeing on the tray. If they cannot spell the object, they can draw a picture of it. The child with the most correct answers wins.

DECORATING IDEAS

Reliving the days of the "Wild West" is a children's playtime favorite. To create a western atmosphere, you can make a tepee by hanging streamers from a central point over the refreshment table and taping the ends of the streamers closely together around the edge of the table between the guests' chairs. There are also many tepee-type tents and playhouses on the market you can buy or borrow. A blanket thrown over a card table makes a cozy tepee, too. Cactus shapes cut from cardboard and painted green can be placed around the room to help set the mood.

Make Indian headband invitations from construction paper and write the party information on a paper "feather." Or, make small "WANTED" posters with a picture of the birthday child on them. Write on the invitation that the guests are "WANTED" to come and celebrate a Wild West Birthday. Don't forget to tell the children to come in costume. Or, you can make costumes at the party. (See "Wild West Costumes," page 42.)

Make a **Totem Pole** by drawing faces on cardboard boxes of graduating sizes, using the largest box as the base. Fasten the boxes on top of each other with a heavy-duty stapler or glue gun. You can also make a **Totem-Pole Centerpiece** by cutting out sections from cardboard egg cartons and gluing them together. (See Diagram 1.) Decorate the totem pole with felt-tip pens, paints, or crayons. Attaching cardboard wings makes it even more realistic. Glue the bottom of the finished totem pole to a flat piece of wood. With adult supervision, these decorations can also be made at the party as part of the party fun.

MUNCHIES

For **Indian Refreshments,** frost the cupcakes and decorate them with faces made from candy, adding black licorice braids; line them up on the table totem-pole style. (See Diagram 2.) For "Cowboy" refreshments, make **Covered Wagons** by frosting ¼ graham cracker and topping it with another ¼ frosted graham cracker, making a wagon bed. Place two large marshmallows, flat sides together, on top of the frosted cracker. Attach round, hard candy wheels with dabs of frosting. Join two animal crackers together with frosting and stand them in front of the wagon. (See Diagram 3.)

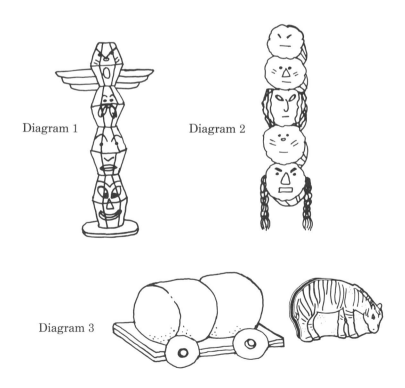

Diagram 1

Diagram 2

Diagram 3

PARTY FUN

Wild West Costumes

Make **Indian Headbands** from paper bags or construction paper by cutting out a long strip of paper (about 25″ by 1½″) and a feather shape. Tape or staple the feather to the band. Measure the band to fit the child's head, remove and staple or tape ends together. Or use paper bags to make **Sheriff's Vests** by cutting armholes and neck openings. (See Diagram 1.) The children can color their vests or headbands with crayons or felt-tip pens. A **Sheriff's Badge** can be colored directly on the vests, or you can cut out construction paper stars prior to the party and let the children color them, then stick them to their vests with a glue stick.

Diagram 1

Cowboy Boot Boogie

Divide the children into teams and have them remove their shoes. Give one pair of adult-size western boots to each team. Place one chair for each team on the opposite side of the room. At the signal to begin, have the first child on each team put on a pair of boots and hurry across the room, around the chair, and back to his or her team. The child must then remove the boots and give them to the next person on his or her team, who repeats the relay. The first team to have each member complete the relay wins.

Fill Your Quiver!

Before the party, hide real feathers, or feathers cut from paper, around the party area. Give each child a brown paper sack for his or her "quiver." At the signal to begin, the children try to find the hidden feathers and put them in their quiver. For extra excitement, have the children give a "war whoop" everytime they find a feather. The child with the most feathers at the end of the game wins.

String That Wampum!

Give each child a shoelace, with one end knotted, and a bowl of large macaroni or wooden beads. At the signal to begin, the children start stringing the beads onto their shoelaces. After the designated time limit is up, the child with the most "wampum" on his or her shoelace wins.

Partner Roundup

Divide the children into pairs. Give each pair a broom and six plastic canning jar rings. One partner holds the broomstick in his or her hands while standing on the broom straws, keeping the bottom of the broom stationary. The other partner stands about 10 feet away and tosses the jar rings to his or her partner, who tries to catch the rings on the broomstick by moving it back and forth. The pair with the most rings on their broomstick wins. Play at least two rounds so each partner gets a chance to "ride" the broom and to try to "lasso" it with the jar rings.

Wide open spaces for active children to enjoy themselves, as well as easy preparation for Mom, make outdoor parties an excellent choice for birthday fun.

Since weather is an unpredictable factor in party success, the key is to be prepared for anything! You may want to schedule an alternate rain date for spring or summer parties. Or, just ask each child to bring an umbrella, golashes, and an extra set of dry clothes for a wet time of wild outdoor activities followed by indoor refreshments.

For parties during the winter months, have children bring snowsuits, hats, mittens, boots, and an extra set of warm clothes. Dressed properly, children should be able to comfortably enjoy snow play for a half an hour or more. Keep a large plastic trash bag by the backdoor where you can put all of the children's wet clothing when they come inside. You may want to borrow some extra snow gear beforehand, just to make sure everyone has adequate protection from the cold. Have another adult in the house with coloring books or simple craft activities for any child who gets too cold and wants to come inside.

DECORATING IDEAS

Other than decorating your refreshment table, there's little need for decorations at an outdoor party. A party tablecloth taped to your refreshment table with a few balloons tied to your backyard fence or trees is all the decorating that's needed.

Invitations for a "sun" party can be written with a felt-tip pen on inexpensive, inflatable beach balls. Or, make a Popsicle® invitation by cutting a rectangular shape out of construction paper, writing the party information on one side, and gluing a clean Popsicle stick on the other. For a "snow" party, write invitations on cut-out construction paper shapes of mittens, snowmen, or snowflakes.

MUNCHIES

For a "sun" party, have lots of ice cold beverages on hand. Cut a watermelon in half and put candles in one of the halves for a "cake." Or, make an **Ice Cream Castle** by removing the carton from a ½ gallon block of ice cream. Quickly scoop spoonfuls of ice cream away from the top edges. (See Diagram 1.) Decorate the castle by pressing candies and a graham cracker drawbridge into the block of ice cream. Make flags by taping triangles of colored paper to wooden picks and inserting them into the top of the castle. (See Diagram 2.) Keep the castle in the freezer until it's time to be served.

Diagram 1   Diagram 2

For a special "snow" party treat, have the children make **Snow Ice Cream** by pouring a small amount of milk over a bowl of clean snow. Add a little vanilla and honey, or brown sugar, to taste. Stir and serve immediately. Or, make **Snow Cones** by putting clean snow into paper cups and pouring thawed, frozen juice concentrate over the ice. Place a straw in each cup. Don't forget to have hot cocoa or cider ready *inside* for warming up!

PARTY FUN IN THE SUN

Chimpanzee Race

Divide the children into two teams that will race in two-person heats. Have the first members of each team spread their feet apart, and then bend over and grab their ankles. At the signal to begin, the two children must walk to a set goal line in this position while keeping their knees stiff. If they let go of their ankles, they must return to the starting point and begin again. The first child to cross the goal line wins the heat. After everyone has had a turn, the team that has won the most heats wins the game.

Melting Madness

Give each child a plastic knife and an ice cube. At the signal to begin, each child puts the ice cube on his or her knife and attempts to hurry to the goal line about 10 feet away. If the ice cube slides off the knife along the way, the child must get the ice cube back on the knife without using his or her hands. For very young children, you may want to use plastic spoons instead of knives. The first child to cross the goal line wins.

Fill The Cup!

Divide the children into two teams. Give each team a bucket (or large bowl) of water and a tablespoon. Set a measuring cup about 10 feet away from each team. At the signal to begin, the first member of each team gets a spoonful of water from the team's bucket and hurries across the yard to pour the spoonful of water into the team's measuring cup. The players then hurry back to their teams and give the spoons to the next team members in line. They then repeat the action. The team who has the most water in their measuring cup at the end of 3 minutes wins.

Vegetable Croquet

This is a fun-filled version of a garden party favorite. It's played like a regular game of croquet, only each child uses a potato instead of a ball—it makes for unpredictable excitement!

Sunshine Suggestions . . .

There are many simple outdoor activities that can be used as party games. If it's warm, a game of water-balloon catch or squirt-gun tag may be the hit of the party. Let the children draw with sidewalk chalk on the driveway, or "paint" the driveway or fence with brushes and plain water. Have a watermelon seed-spitting contest or play volleyball with balloons!

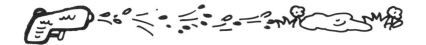

PARTY FUN IN THE SNOW

Rainbow Snow Search

Before the party, make several trays of different-colored ice cubes, using water mixed with several drops of food color. Right before the guests arrive, scatter the colored cubes in the snow in the outdoor party area. To play the game, give each child a plastic bag or pail. Ask the children to search for all of the "rainbow snow" they can find. The child with the greatest number of ice cubes at the end of the designated time limit wins.

The Snowflake Gallery

Give children spray bottles filled with colored ice water and let them turn a backyard snowdrift into a work of art by "painting" it. Older children will also enjoy using large brushes and tempera paints. You can give a prize to the most imaginative work of art, or just let the children make a group-effort gallery.

Snow Shovel Relay

This game is a great way to get your driveway shoveled! Divide the children into two teams. With a shovel, mark a line down the middle of a snow-covered driveway or walkway. Give each child a children's snow shovel, dustpan, or sandbox shovel. At the signal to begin, each team tries to clear the snow away from "their side" of the line. Make it clear that putting snow on the other team's side is against the rules. The first team to clear its side of snow wins.

Snowtime Suggestions . . .

Don't forget simple snowtime pleasures such as a snowman-building contest or snowball-throwing competition, or the fun of making "angels" in a snowbank. Or, design snow castles instead of sand castles, using plastic cups and bowls as molds. Try making igloos with loaf pans for molds!

THEME PARTIES